THE SPIRIT
IS MOVING

THE SPIRIT IS MOVING

FESTO KIVENGERE

COMMUNITY CHRISTIAN MINISTRIES
MOSCOW, IDAHO

Published by Community Christian Ministries
P.O. Box 9754, Moscow, Idaho 83843
208.883.0997 | www.ccmbooks.org

Festo Kivengere, *The Spirit Is Moving*.
Copyright © 1979 by African Enterprise, Spokane, Washington. Used
by permission.

First edition published 1976 by Africa Christian Press, Achimota,
Ghana. Second edition published in 1979 by African Enterprise.
Third edition published in 2019 by Community Christian Ministries.

Edited by Lisa Just.
Cover and interior design by Valerie Anne Bost.
Cover photo by Christiana Hale, instagram.com/cbhalephotography.

Printed in the United States of America.

19 20 21 22 23 24 25 26 27   9 8 7 6 5 4 3 2 1

CONTENTS

CHAPTER 1

GOD IS ALIVE

I want to tell you, the Lord is alive! The Holy Spirit is in business these days, reconciling men and women to God and to each other. Christ is healing our wounds and touching us where no one else could have touched us.

Some years ago, we had a mission in the city of Dar es Salaam in Tanzania. Our team was invited by some Christian brethren in the city. When we got there, we were taken by surprise. We thought the inviting team was made up of those from certain Protestant churches, but we found the main body of the committee was made up of Roman Catholics!

We had the greatest experience of our lives, preaching biblical messages, sharing the Lord in Roman Catholic churches, and seeing men and women coming to Jesus Christ. It was beautiful. It was the Lord. I found myself preaching three times, at one mass after another, in the beautiful church of Saint Peter's in Dar es Salaam, and that was my first experience of preaching at a service called a mass.

I am an Anglican, and we do not do things in the same way as the Catholics. We have our way of doing things, just as others have their ways. When we arrived at the church, we found it packed with seven hundred people. As we came into the sanctuary, the priest whispered to me, "Festo, these people are not used to preaching; they are used to mass and liturgy." This was the priest in charge. He turned around, beaming, and said, "Therefore, preach, brother, and don't worry about the time. If they get tired, the door is open, they can go home."

No one went home. It was beautiful. I preached at one service after another, and the church was full. The last service they held in Latin which I did not understand, but I preached anyway, and God was doing great things. That evening our mission ended in a stadium. We had a very large crowd of people representing: all the churches, and the Roman Catholic cardinal was sitting by my side. There were three preachers that afternoon, and when we finished he stood up to conclude the meeting and prayed beautifully. He praised God for what was happening. He was a wonderful man, and we loved him, and he loved Christ. The Holy Spirit is in business, and there is no question of looking back.

MIGHTY MOVEMENT

Let me take you to another area. You may have heard about Indonesia, and what God is doing there. They have experienced a mighty movement of God, and because they knew we had experienced God's working in our own area in East Africa for more than forty years, they wanted us to go there and share the goodness of the Lord.

We arrived, and do you know what we saw? A tremendous army of men and women who love Jesus. Thousands of Muslims have become Christians. I was preaching at a meeting, and when I was through a gentleman came and took my hand. He was excited, and he said to me, "Do you know, Festo, if we had met six months ago, I would not have hesitated to kill you because I was a fanatic Muslim and I hated Christians. But now I love you as a brother." And he put his arms round me and said, "I love Jesus."

I said, "Well, how did it happen? As you were such a staunch, fighting Muslim, who preached to you?"

He said, "No one. I was sleeping in my house in my Muslim village, and at midnight someone woke me up, and I heard him say to me, 'I am Jesus, and I want you to believe in Me.' I shook my head and said, 'I am a Muslim, and I do not know anything about You.' He repeated, 'Yes, I know you know nothing about Me, and that is why I have come.' I said, 'But I do not know anything. How can I believe? I do not understand. I read the Koran; I do not know the holy book of the Christians.' He said, 'All right, tomorrow morning get up, and go six miles, and you will meet a man. Tell him what has happened tonight, and he will tell you who I am.'

"In the morning I got up, went six miles, and met a man, and I told him what had happened the night before. The man was a Christian. He took his New Testament out, and he told me who Jesus was, and about His love on the cross, and the power of His resurrection.

"I bowed and said, 'Thank you indeed. Thank you very much, sir. You have told me who He is. I saw Him last night, and now I believe in Him.' I went home rejoicing, gathered the villagers, all Muslims, and gave my testimony straight away. Since then, two of my Muslim villages have become Christian."

FULL OF JOY

I was riding with a young man who was absolutely full of joy, bubbling over with infectious vitality. He said he was so full of spiritual hunger he wanted to stay with me so that we could share and pray together. We did, and we spent two days together. One day he told me his story.

"Do you see? Look at my neck." He said, "In December I tried to commit suicide. That is the scar you see here. I gambled all my money. I was a victim of overdrinking. My family had no support; my poor wife did not know what to do. I had two lovely children, but I could not support them.

"My life became so burdened and guilty that in the end I thought I should not live any longer. One night I left my wife in bed, and I went into the next room and put a rope round my neck to take away my life. But my wife knew I was not well. She woke up, came rushing into the room, and found me hanging on the rope. She cried, and the neighbors came, cut the rope, and rescued me before I died. The story got to the police, and so the police took me and put me into protective custody to protect me against myself, because I was going to destroy myself.

"I spent two days at the police station in a cell, crying my heart out, seeking means to destroy myself without success. I became so angry that I wept in bitterness. Then in the end I got tired, and I put my hand in my pocket and there was a little book. It was a New Testament. I do not know who put it there."

This man was not a Muslim; he was a nominal member of the Reformed Church of Indonesia.

"I took it and began to read, with my tears coming down. I had hardly finished two verses when the Lord of the New Testament came into the cell. Immediately, what I never expected happened. Jesus entered into this miserable heart of mine, and it was too good for me to believe it. Jesus kept saying, 'I love you,' and I kept shaking my head and saying, 'You cannot love me, I hate myself, I want to kill myself.' And He said, 'I love you; I died for you.' 'But I want to die.' 'You need not die, because I died for you.'

"Slowly I began to realize that He loved me. And, you know, my heart began to experience a completely new release. Immediately the Spirit of God brought Christ into my heart in a way that I never knew could happen. I was so full of joy that I was weeping and laughing and shouting and singing. The policeman came to see what had happened, whether I had now gone mad completely. He opened the door and looked in, and he could not believe his eyes. He went and called another officer, and they came and looked in. They saw me dancing about and singing. They decided to keep me in for a day just to make sure. So they kept me in. After a day they called me out.

"I came out and stood before the two officers, and I said to them with tears of joy, 'Jesus has come to me. I came here miserable. I was going to kill myself; I was so lost, and my life was a living death. But Jesus came and loved me, and now I am different. I love Him.' I was laughing and singing, and the policeman said, 'He is all right. Go home.' So I went home, and I told my wife, who could hardly believe it. I gathered the people in the village and told them, and I have not stopped. It is two months now."

And he could not stop. He was seeking to go into the Bible Institute where I was preaching so that he could enter into full-time ministry. He told me, "I want to tell all the young people of Indonesia that Jesus can put the broken pieces together." When you looked at that man and saw the scar where the rope had nearly killed him, it was like seeing a man who had come to life again. He was vibrating with vitality. He was no longer seeking to die. He was seeking to live. Jesus lets people live again.

Then I moved from Indonesia. I did not like to go away; the young people were so on fire. They are beautiful singers, and they used to come and sing for me. I left them reluctantly and went to the Solomon Islands.

ALIVE CHURCH

Now you have not heard what is happening in the Solomon Islands, but it is a tremendous thing. For the last three years, the Church has become so alive that services are filled with people one and one-half hours before the time. On my arrival from the plane, they gave me twenty minutes to wash my face and come and preach.

They had built extensions on the church to make room for the crowd. What I saw was wonderful. As I came near the church, the singing was so powerful that I thought the roof would almost be blown off! The extensions were packed, and there were twice as many people on the road as there were inside. I managed to get in the church.

People were singing and rejoicing, some were clapping, and others were standing up and giving their testimony.

I even thought there was no need for preaching. I could have sat and enjoyed the wonderful happenings. The Holy Spirit was preaching. Why bother with a preacher? Anyway, I did say a few things, and I got excited too, because the Spirit of God blessed me through them. I simply opened my mouth, and every word I said they loved. The gathering was full of the Spirit of the Lord, and they were spiritually hungry. When the Spirit of God fills a person, he begins to long for Jesus more and more. He longs for more of Heaven, and for more of His love.

I spent three weeks with those dear people, and I was preaching three times a day for three weeks. The congregations averaged 2,500, and particularly young people were all over the place with the freshness of Jesus. Talk about obedience to Jesus! They did not leave any stone unturned. Lives were completely turned inside-out and right-side-up. There was no longer the usual sort of halfhearted Christianity. Instead, it was exciting and beautiful and wonderful.

HIGH SCHOOL

I went to one high school to speak to 700 young people. It was a government school, and they invited me to speak to them in the evening. The whole place was packed; Roman Catholics, Protestants of all kinds, and those who worship the spirits of their ancestors were all there, and I started speaking. That evening it was supposed to be a rather quiet meeting, and I was not supposed even to give an invitation because this was a public school.

When I was through, the students refused to go. They stayed there, and I said to them, "Will you please go to your dormitories?" It was a big boarding school. They would not go. I said, "Do you have questions to ask?" They started asking questions, and some of them that night came to the Lord.

When the Holy Spirit comes like the wind, He blows our fences down, and before we know what is happening, we find ourselves embracing one another. When we were in Dar es Salaam, a senior Roman Catholic came to my colleague and said with a simplicity that was childlike, "You know, I do not know much of the Bible. You fellows seem to know a little more. Would you mind if I come every morning to your room for a little fellowship so that I may get acquainted with my Bible more?" Is not that wonderful! He was a senior man, vicar general over a big area. What a humility! He came every morning into our room to have fellowship so that he might get more of the Bible before he went preaching. It was a beautiful job which was done by the Holy Spirit. The Holy Spirit irons out all wrinkles, all the fences go, the fire of God burns them all, and we are introduced to one another through Jesus' cross, and, when we are like that, we love one another.

When the Holy Spirit comes, it does not matter whether it is in a Catholic church, a Presbyterian church, or a Baptist church. People are people, and God loves to bless them. And when He blesses them, the prayer book, whatever book you use, the liturgy, the songs, they become alive. They become alive and fresh. There is joy, there is blessing, there is relaxation. It is beautiful. The Bible begins to speak, and lips also move quickly, witnessing to the glory of Jesus Christ.

CHAPTER 2

CHRIST AND THE HOLY SPIRIT

Let us consider together the Holy Spirit, because without Him there is no Christianity. We tend, when we hear about the blessed Comforter, to put Him over there; and put the Lord Jesus over there; and God the Father over in another corner somewhere. Of course, this is confusion. The Lord Jesus remains an ideal at a distance from you, until the Agent introduces you to Him. The tremendous liberating reality of His truth and the beauty of the New Testament remain a strange story until the Holy Spirit breathes over it. It is, therefore, His blessed work today to bring us effectually into the amazing realities of what we profess and possess.

Jesus Christ is that wonderful Liberator, the One whom we call Lord. But His Lordship remains words, and only words, until the Holy Spirit comes and introduces us into the presence of the cross of our Lord and Saviour. The mighty work on Calvary's cross, the blood shed which speaks better messages to guilty hearts than that of Abel, remains strange talk, just meaningless phrases, until the blessed Holy Spirit comes. Then the cross becomes, not a place of tragedy, but a mighty place of liberation, of fullness, an open Heaven, the embracing hands of the almighty love. That is the work of the blessed Holy Spirit.

Sin also remains just talk about ethics and morals, until the Holy Spirit comes. Then sin appears in its sinfulness, and we find ourselves caught red-handed in His revealing light. Then redeeming love comes out in its glorious, all-embracing power.

Things we had forgotten come up in His light, and we are shocked. Sins we had glossed over are brought to our minds, and we are convicted. Truths we had forgotten come back with amazing power. Who is doing this? The blessed Holy Spirit. We cannot produce conviction of sin. It comes when the blessed Comforter refocuses our attention upon the Lord. Then, in the glare of that amazing Presence, we discover things we did not see before.

NO POLICEMEN

But perhaps some of you regard the Holy Spirit as a policeman. Some of you are scared of Him. You think that if you do something wrong, He comes and says, "This is the law of the land," grabs you, as it were, by the neck, and you are in custody, in the dock. No! the New Testament never says that. The Holy Spirit is not a policeman; He is the Friend of the guilty. That is why He is the Comforter. The policeman is not a comforter when he arrests you under the law. You don't feel comforted: you begin to tremble.

One day I was driving, and I passed a car, crossing the yellow lines. I had hardly finished with the yellow line, when before me I saw a policeman. I began to tremble. I was alive until he came, and then I was dead!

That is exactly what the law does. "The letter kills, but the Spirit gives life," says Paul. The appearance of the Holy Spirit never makes you feel dead. The law takes you by the neck; that is its purpose. The Holy Spirit uses the law to bring you into a realization of exactly what you are like: weak and feeble, unable to do what you want to do, guilty from inside out.

But the blessed Holy Spirit is not a policeman. He is the Friend of the guilty. He simply convicts in order to liberate. He never shows you your sin without showing you your Saviour. That is why, in the New Testament, repentance and rejoicing go together, not apart. As soon as you are convicted by the Holy Spirit, you see Jesus, your Redeemer. He convicts you to release you and to set you free. He shows you your hunger and your emptiness, and immediately He opens your eyes to see the unlimited riches in Jesus Christ.

That is why in the Holy Spirit, Jesus Christ becomes a beautiful Saviour, a glorious King on the throne, holding out all that Heaven has—for you and for me.

POWER AT PENTECOST

What happened on the day of Pentecost?

Here was a group of men, Peter and John and James. They were only ordinary people who stood together in the upper room praying for the power promised by the Lord. "Wait here. You are too weak to face the world. Wait here," Jesus said. "I am going up above. I am entering Glory." Then from that glory He poured out on them His own Holy Spirit.

He had said earlier, "Out of those who believe in Him are going to flow rivers of living water" (John 7:38–39), and John comments: "He spoke about the Holy Spirit who as yet had not been given, because Christ had not yet been glorified." I want you to connect these wonderful things: the Holy Spirit and the glorification of the Lord.

The Holy Spirit comes when God has glorified His Son in the right hand of the throne, in the center of all the blessings of Heaven, so that everything in Heaven is at His command. Angels stand amazed, seeing the entire heavens, all the blessings in the heavenly places, are now at His disposal.

But so many of us are like Jacob: God is ready to bless, but we are unblessable! Some of us, of course, are too good to be blessed! Some of us are too strong to be blessed. We need a touch which is going to cripple us, so that we can cling and be blessed.

So unbroken is my nature, that I go round mourning because I am not blessed, as if the New Testament did not make it clear that He died to bless me; and He rose to bless me; that He was glorified to bless me; that He came down in power to bless me. It is very clear. And yet we are not always blessed, because we are difficult to bless. Some of us are morally so slippery that the Holy Spirit cannot catch us. We are just like a slippery fish: He touches here—we are there; He touches there—we are over here; we keep slipping through His hand, refusing to be brought to the reality of what we are. That is to act like a slippery fish.

I want to tell you that the Holy Spirit is busy in our lives, and He intends to bless all of us by sorting us out, by clarifying things. Do you realize that every truth, every exposition, every preaching has two aims?—to glorify the Lord and to clarify our confused minds.

I know there are many serious-minded Christians who think that to hang endlessly under conviction is a sign of humility. The Holy Spirit will convict you sufficiently so that you may see the Word Jesus; the Holy Spirit will show you your sin so that you may repent of it—not that you may sit on it. You go on scratching your head and lamenting, "Now, why did I act meanly like that? Why? and Why? and Why?"

But you are asking the wrong question. It is not, "Why did I act in a mean way to my brother?" You acted in a mean way, and that's that. What do you need? You need to say to the Lord, "Thank you, blessed Comforter, that you have shown me my meanness in order that it may be taken away." No more wasting of time going in circles.

He said you were jealous of your brother. The question is not, "Why was I jealous?" You were jealous. When the Holy Spirit has shown you that you were jealous, it is His blessed work—it is His priority number one—to set you free from it.

TO THE CROSS

He sets you free, not that you may linger on in the sin, but that you may present the jealousy to the cross. This is where He keeps pointing us all the time. He takes us from our emptiness, our weakness and feebleness, and He leads us to the amazing place of His bountiful grace.

At Pentecost, the first disciples stood trembling in fear and frustration. Many of them had suffered from sin, and they were still suffering from sins of doubt and confusion. Who could restore Peter from the haunting awareness that three times he had denied Him whom he loved? Tell me, what teacher on earth could have come and explained carefully so that Peter was no longer confused as to why he denied Him whom he followed? Is not that a deep confusion? How do you disentangle this man? How do you really get him out of this terrible mix-up? Yet he came out. You meet him on the day of Pentecost: he is completely out. He is no longer a halfhearted Peter still suffering from the hangover of his guilt.

Do you know there are many of us, even those who have listened to the messages of forgiveness and the mighty work of the Holy Spirit, and the lordship of Christ, who still carry with us hangovers. "Yes, I came to the Lord last night asking for forgiveness, but I am not rejoicing in it. I still have a hangover. I know He died for me, of course. But how do you clarify it?" Well, my dear friend, we are entering into the simple but deep secret of how people can repent, and rejoice, and live, and say so. This is all there is to it.

I want to take you to a picture which I love, because it may help us to clarify this matter. The crowd of Christians who gathered on the day of Pentecost were just like you and me. Their hearts and minds had a lot of hangovers and doubts, like Thomas. They were bad-tempered, like John and James, the sons of thunder. We have all sorts of temperaments, and we need to stand in the exposure of our wonderful, dynamic Redeemer. Of course, He knows you, with all your psychological makeup, as He does me. But He does not come here to analyze us, and leave us trembling, as it were, in a psychiatrist's room. He comes here to show us what we are in the light of who He is.

The Holy Spirit came on the day of Pentecost. What did He do? He came, sent by the mighty, risen Lord. He knew how His people—those men and women—were. They were still ignorant about what Jesus had told them: "I am the vine; you are the branches." Had they entered into its joy? No, it remained a figure of speech.

Jesus breathed the Holy Spirit into them after the resurrection. Did they receive Him? It remained a bit of a metaphor until He came. He was sent purposely to unconfuse the confused, to clothe the naked, to liberate the prisoners, to make weak men and women live. And I believe that you, too, are going to live as you expose yourself to Him.

CHAPTER 3

CHRIST THE GIVER OF LIFE

I was away from home preaching, and I had a letter from my wife. In the letter, she said something that was very searching. She thanked me for my letter to her, and she said, "Before I got your letter, which was very encouraging, I had already had an interview with my Saviour about my present problem, and He has seen me through."

I was miles away from my wife, and I cannot tell you what good that letter did to me. There she was alone, and she had had that interview about her problem, and He had seen her through it. If she had to wait for my poor letters, she would have to wait for days for them to reach her, but she had Jesus there by her side. Right in her heart there was the One she needed. What a practical Saviour we have!

I want to point you to Jesus Christ. I could tell you testimony after testimony of what He has meant in my home and what happens when a person comes afresh to Jesus Christ. When He comes, it makes all the difference in the world—there is a melting of the heart, a lifting of the burden, a new comfort, and a drying of tears.

In John, chapter 11, we read about a little village called Bethany. Every time the Lord

Jesus was tired of the questions in Jerusalem, he used to go to Bethany. There was
nothing spectacular about the village. It
was an ordinary little Jewish village, but
in it lived two sisters and a brother, very
ordinary people, and their home was much
like yours and mine. We do not read that
in it there was much of this world's goods,
but time and again that home had the presence of the Saviour in it. Jesus went there
when He was tired. Martha, Mary, and
Lazarus served and enjoyed Him. What an
exceptional privilege for that small town
to receive Jesus whenever He was rejected
in Jerusalem! He would go to Bethany, and
what sweet peace there must have been in
that little village when the Saviour was giv-
en a bed in a corner of the house! Martha
and Mary would sit together perhaps and
rejoice, for Heaven was in that home.

DARK HOUR

Well, one day the people were upset. Lazarus had been taken ill. The illness went from bad to worse until, as we read in verse 14, Jesus said plainly, "Lazarus is dead." What a terrible thing! Lazarus had died. He was the only hope of the two sisters. Some of you have been through that dark hour when everything is absolutely against you. Yes, some sickness has developed into death, and the brother has died, and the sisters have been left half-dead. They were in that world of emptiness; nothing could fill the place of the dear brother.

Do any of you feel like that? You have friends to comfort you. Many came to comfort Mary and Martha, but they only wept, and the two sisters wept because that was all they could do. None could give them comfort. Read psalms, speak sweet words, tell stories of old, counsel if you like, but they do not really help. Martha and Mary wept and wept. It was a terrible situation, the darkest hour for the two sisters and for Bethany. The whole village changed; no longer were there any songs of praise, no longer sweet smiles, only darkness and despair.

That "Bethany" can be anywhere. It can be a home where the situation has got completely out of hand. You look at it and you look again, and there is no ray of hope for that situation, for that broken relationship. All looks dark. No one seems to understand your situation. You feel you are desolate in a world of loneliness.

Yes, it was dark in Bethany. The situation had gone completely wrong. Everything was turned completely upside down, and these situations take place in homes, and in churches. They begin in individual lives. These are not strange situations—they are very common in life.

If you say, "I don't know anything of that," you will be an extraordinary human being. But if you are like me, you have in one way or another tasted something of the situation in Bethany. Not necessarily death, but deadness in circumstances, death in business, death in money matters, death between friends, death in broken relationships, death in some darkness which has come into the home. Yes, we know about that.

It was indeed hopeless in Bethany until Jesus said, "Lazarus is dead…But let us go to him." Then hope came. And this hope came literally walking on foot. Hope came to Bethany walking in a bodily form at the very moment when the two sisters needed Him.

He came to Bethany. Love brought Him all the way. He loved Martha and Lazarus and Mary, and He came to them.

Martha went to meet Jesus with a hopeless situation, a heart overrun with pain, grief, and despair. She stands before Him and speaks out her heart: "Dear Lord Jesus, had You been here, my brother would never have died."

RAY OF HOPE

Jesus replied, "Your brother will rise again." This gave a ray of hope, but Martha was not really comforted. She knew that her brother could never come back again. Nothing anyone said to comfort her could change the circumstances. I have spoken with people who said, "You do not understand. The circumstances in which I find myself can never be changed.

You don't understand my husband. If you knew what sort of man he is, you would never talk to me like that." Or, "You do not know my wife and the temperament she has! If you understood, you would never think that my home could enjoy that fellowship—far from it."

But Jesus when He came to Bethany knew the situation. He knew what had happened even before Lazarus had died. He knew. He knew it all and that is why He came. He knew the full story, and He came to remedy the situation.

Martha came moaning, "If you had been here, Master, this darkness, this fear, these red eyes, these broken hearts, this whole hopelessness would not be here."

Is there a situation in your church which you think has gone beyond remedy? Are there such things in your family?

But the Word Jesus has come now.

"Martha, your brother will rise again. He will come back to life."

Then Martha answered, "I know."

"What do you know, Martha?"

She knew the doctrine of the resurrection.

"I know that my brother, in some unknown future, will come back to life. I know the doctrine of the resurrection that people will rise again in the distant future."

The immediate need was for her brother to come back to life, and then the fear would be gone; then there would be joy. But instead of taking Jesus' word in the immediate present, she was looking to that distant future day. The Master had not come for that. He had not come to preach to Martha a doctrine of the future. She did not need that. A mere doctrine makes us more tired, when we are already tired.

JESUS IS PRACTICAL

Jesus is more practical than that. He sees our circumstances and gives us the water of life and never troubles tired people with complicated doctrines. The Lord Jesus was very practical. He said, "I am the resurrection and the life. Martha, I'm not speaking of the future. I am right here in front of you. In the immediate present I am the resurrection, because you need resurrection for your brother. I am the life, because you need life for your brother. Why not let Me bring him to life? I am what you need.'"

Jesus wants to be what you need. Martha believed and went back and told her sister, Mary, "The Master has come and is calling for you."

What Martha said to Mary is what the Holy Spirit is saying to you even as you read this message. "The Master has come, and He is particularly calling for you." The Master knows you individually, and He knows the things which are making you miserable—the things which wring your life, which press upon your broken heart, which take the fellowship and the sweetness of the Lord from you and your husband or wife. The Master is come, the Master is here, and He is particularly calling for you.

He did not send an angel to Bethany. He came Himself because He knew the situation could not be remedied except through Him who is the life, the resurrection, the revival.

You probably know that after Jesus had dealt with Martha, He raised Lazarus from the dead. I know that you are probably concerned about some or your friends or relatives who are not saved.

You are going to keep them in their graves unless you mean business with Jesus Christ.

Martha kept Lazarus, her beloved brother, in the grave all the time she was arguing and reasoning and doubting. It took the Lord Jesus quite some time to convince the living Martha that He had come to raise Lazarus from the grave. It takes Jesus sometimes a long time to convince Christians of their need, but it takes Him a much shorter time to bring the dead souls to life.

"Martha, I am the resurrection, I am the life. I am the One you need—I am the only One who can change the situation."

Perhaps you are wanting to know now what you should do. Do what they did.

AT THE GRAVE

"Where have you laid him?" Jesus asked.

There were neighbors who came to comfort Martha and Mary. Do you know where they stopped? In the house. They did not go to the grave. And do you know where the trouble was? It was at the grave. The tears were in the house, but the whole cause of those tears was in the grave. Anyone who wanted to give help in that home of Bethany had to deal with the situation in the grave. Most of the comforters sat in the house. They did not go far enough. Not my Lord Jesus! When He comes, He never goes halfway.

He said, "Where have you laid him?" He wants to go to the very bottom of your problem. He wants to get at the cause so that He may heal it.

They said, "Lord, come and see." Would you like to take the Saviour by the hand now and say, "Master, come and see into my home…into my money…into my relationship with this fellow, with my neighbor. Master, come and look into this muddle— it is not a respectable sight." Immediately, you say, "Come and look into my life—it is not respectable." He walks in, and He makes it right.

Then the Bible tells us that Jesus wept. Not tears of sorrow, but tears of love. Those around said, "Look how he loved him." Would you like Jesus to start looking at your problem? His tears of love are for you.

Finally, Jesus had to tell the people to take away the stone. Some of us may need to take away the stone, in repentance— however indecent and stinking things may be, causing shame and grief to those who know us. Be not be ashamed. Jesus says to you, "Repent. Take away the stone."

The Lord Jesus said, "If you trust Me for it, you will see the glory of God come out of that terrible situation—out of that stinking grave."

Would you like to see the glory coming out of your terrible situation? It will come when you allow Jesus to look deep into your life. Will you even now take away the stone?

CHAPTER 4

CHRIST THE RENEWER

In John 8:1–12 we have the record of the fragmented and broken life of a religious woman. She belonged to Israel; and hardly any Israelite could be regarded as irreligious. Here is a human being—and let us not call her a sinner, for the New Testament does not call her that but "a woman who was caught in the act of adultery."

Then we have the religious leaders, the Pharisees and the scribes. They were concerned about putting men and women right; their responsibility was to see that every Israelite was in right relationship with God—the pure God, the holy God, the perfect God. They used the law, and the law was correct, because the law was the standard for Israel. The scribes represented those who had studied the law carefully—doctors of theology; the Pharisees represented the very conservative orthodoxy among the Jews, the keepers of the law.

So they caught this woman in the act of adultery. How they did it we do not know. However, that is what we are told. This woman had missed the mark badly, and had been taken advantage of by her weakness and by humanity. Other human beings used her like a thing, exploiting her for their own ends. Sin is always an exploitation and misuse of humanity. Here was a life without a target, a life without a center, a life corroded, empty of meaning, frozen and ashamed of itself.

Tell me, who on earth could put those pieces together? The law? Let us see whether it could. The law goes to this woman, and the law—as represented by the scribes and the Pharisees—is angry. Their standards are high—morality could not have been more zealous—and they were going to deal with this case. Here was a broken woman, corroded by her sin, shattered by repeated defeats, weakened to the core, one who could not even love herself. When you fail and fail again and again, you hate yourself. This is the effect sin has.

DRAGGED TO THE TEMPLE

The religious representatives went to the woman and arrested her. They dragged her—I don't know how far, perhaps from the suburbs of Jerusalem, perhaps from the areas of the city which were notoriously known for looseness, where people of the streets, the prostitutes, lived. They dragged this person, and they brought her—of all places!—into the temple. Now that was a terrible scare for a person caught in adultery, to be brought into the temple, without a sacrifice. Nothing protecting! No refuge at all!

Where do you look when you are brought into the open like that? Do you look at yourself? Do you have anywhere to look, any comfort, any consolation? Nothing at all! Here was a person completely frozen. The authority that took her had no authority to renew her. The best they could do was to treat her like an object—a thing. The woman was, in their eyes, only a sinner. They dragged her into the temple purposely to use her as an exhibit to catch Jesus Christ. Just an exhibit!

They made her stand in front of the gathering of people who were listening to Jesus that morning, in the midst—not at the side! In the center, with all eyes gazing upon her, was that poor woman, bearing all the piercing looks of the crowd and the aloofness of the scribes and the Pharisees.

As she stood in the center, they accused her, saying, "Moses told us that such cases should be stoned to death: what do you say?" And the Master never looked at the woman.

The Lord Jesus turned away from her and from them. He looked upon the ground. I cannot tell you why, but I know He was the loving Saviour; I know that it was He who invited Zacchaeus, and it was He who told us the story of the prodigal son, and ultimately it was He who hung on the cross of Calvary where blood, sweat, and love flowed down. He looked down to save an already embarrassed sinner extra embarrassment, in order that this poor woman might be spared another burden, another crushing wave. She had had enough; now she needed to be renewed.

Then He looked up, turned to the crowd, and said, "Anyone among you who has never committed the same sin—or desired to commit that sin—let him be the first person to throw the condemning stone." But remember His teaching: He said, "If you look at a person and desire, you have already committed the sin in your heart."

He looked down a second time, I believe to save the accusers embarrassment. For His words, His light, had pierced through the gloom; and the self-righteous who thought they were better than she became aware that they were no better than the woman after all. Immediately, when they were brought into the X-ray of the presence of Jesus Christ, they discovered they had made a big mistake; they had become blind to what sin was about. They had thought that sin was a mere external act, instead of an inward principle of going wrong. They discovered that they, too, were as guilty and as bad inside as the woman was bad outside.

One after another, the accusers walked out of the room. Quietly, from the eldest to the youngest, they disappeared. Only the crowd which was listening, and the Lord Jesus, and the woman remained. The woman was still standing in the center, but there had been a change of atmosphere. No more judgment, no more condemnation, but renewal.

NOT CHEAP LOVE

Renewal always begins in the presence of Jesus Christ. The presence of Jesus Christ goes deeper than any Ten Commandments can ever go. The love which came all the way from Heaven and refused to be put off is not cheap love. It is not going to be put off, whatever the cost. It stoops to the desperate case of a human being, thoroughly guilty, thoroughly filthy, deeply unclean, repeatedly defeated, hating herself, hated by society.

Let me tell you something very deep. That eternal, pure love decided to take its place by her side. It was as if Jesus crossed over to her. This is how renewal begins. It does not begin when you are pleading your case. The woman never did—there was nothing to plead. In the presence of Jesus, you and I are completely dumbfounded.

If you still have excuses to use, you are at a distance from the Presence. If you still have some people you compare yourself with, you are at a distance; in His presence there is no comparing. We all look the same. The accusers and the accused were all the same. The only difference was, He was there; and in His presence the woman stood, and there the beginning of renewal started.

You may have never been caught in that kind of external mess in which this woman was trapped, but what an inward mess we all have been in! What about the realm of our thoughts, dispositions, resentments, hatreds? There we are no better than she.

The Lord Jesus turned to her and said, "Woman, where are Your accusers?" The word "woman" in that verse is the word He used of His mother: "Woman, what have I to do with you?" It has the sense in Greek, I believe, of "lady"—"My dear lady, where are your accusers? No one condemns you?" And she answered for the first time: "No one, Lord." In the presence of the Renewer, caught in that warmth of life, and with the light piercing through the gloom, melting the mountains of her guilt, she begins to experience release and renewal, to the extent that now she dares to speak. She can now open her mouth, encouraged by the Renewer. Accepted in the Beloved, she begins to accept herself.

She says, "No one, Lord," and I believe she said "No one" with a sense of wonder. "No one! I did not expect it! I expected everyone to condemn me. I was already condemning myself. Everyone really should condemn me. I am not suggesting that they shouldn't. I am surprised. No one."

Then she added that beautiful word: "Lord." The wonderful word, the new discovery: "I am in good hands." Renewal begins in His presence.

Renewal, then, means you and I looking at Him with a sense of gratitude, excitement, and wonder that we are not condemned. We look at Him and say, "It's You, Lord, who has stopped the condemnation! It's You, Lord, because I'm standing in Your presence! No one, Lord. No voice can condemn." We are talking about Him who died on the cross of Calvary, the price He paid for the renewal. He stood where the woman stood. He refused to condemn, because He was going to bear the condemnation. He went all the way to Calvary for that woman—and for you and for me. And in going that way, He made it very clear that you and I can experience continued renewal in His Presence.

IN HIS PRESENCE

I believe that as you read these words you are in His presence. That woman heard the Lord say, "Nor do I condemn you, my dear lady. Go and sin no more," or, "Go, and do not sin again."

Can you imagine those beautiful words of the Renewed, the power and the authority? "I am not here to condemn. I did not come to condemn already condemned people: I know they have had enough already. I did not come to make the burden heavier. I came to remove the burden. I did not come to make Christians utterly miserable and dejected. I came to usher them into the presence of the life-giving God. I am come that the prisoner may lose his chain, that the poor may become rich in Me, that the lost may find the way back to the Father, that the haters may be filled with love, that the burdened may feel light like little birds with wings. I am come not to condemn, but to give remission."

The remission He gives comes from Calvary. "Go, and do not sin again." The woman listened to those words: "Go? You mean I am released?"

"Of course you are! You can go home. You didn't come here; you were brought here. But now I give you permission to go. You no longer need people to drag you. Now I give you the power and the authority to become alive again."

The woman was excited—and then she heard another word, "And do not sin again. I am not giving you permission to sin, because that would corrode you again."

Christians make a big mistake when they think that talk about grace may encourage a Christian to sin! Grace never encourages

a man or a woman to sin. It saves men
and women from sin, for we are "saved by
grace." If I think, because God is gracious,
I can commit another sin, I am absolutely
a stranger to grace. Grace is love I do not
deserve. This woman hears, "Go home, and
do not sin anymore."

"Can you trust me, Lord Jesus? Is it pos-
sible to trust a character like mine to go into
the city and sin no more?"

The woman went away with the powerful words of the Saviour who died on the
cross, because it was the same Saviour who
went to Calvary. This was liberating love;
this was His releasing power; this was the
same One who hung on the cross of Calvary. When He speaks His word to you, "Go
home, and sin no more," those words become the very power to give you authority
not to sin. They become a source of power,

a dynamic in you to enable you to walk,
and not to sin.

CHRIST THE LIBERATOR

In 2 Corinthians chapter 5, the apostle Paul is answering people who were criticizing him, and had actually misjudged him, and interpreted his excitement and enthusiasm as meaning he was out of his mind; and this is the way he answers. He shows them what the liberating grace of Christ can do in their lives. He says:

For us, there is no escape from the love of Christ; for we have reached the certainty that one died for all men: and if Christ died for all, we cannot escape the conclusion that all were dead. So He died for us; and therefore all through life men must no longer live for themselves, but must live for Him who for them died and was raised to life again.

The consequence of all this is that from now on we evaluate no man on purely human standards. There was a time when we evaluated Christ by human standards. We no longer do so, for when a man is in Christ, he becomes entirely a new creation. And the whole process is due to the action of God who through Christ turned our enmity to Himself into friendship, and who gave us the task of helping others to accept that friendship.

The fact is that God was acting in Christ to turn the world's enmity to Himself into friendship; that He was not holding men's sins against them, and that He placed upon us the privilege of taking to men who are hostile to Him this offer of His friendship. (2 Cor. 5:14–19, Barclay)

In the center of this New Testament passage is Christ the Liberator.

WE ARE TOO SMALL

First, what does Christ liberate us from? Paul knew from experience, not just theologically, that to become your own center is to empty your humanity of its meaning.

There has never been an emptier life than the one which has itself as its center. You take the throne of your personality and sit on it, and you appear conspicuously too small! It was never meant to be *your* throne. We were created in God's image, not in our own image. Therefore, whenever I take the center of my personality and sit on it, I am out of place. I am simply too small for the throne of that personality. I cannot meet my own desires. That is why you find there is a danger that the very gifts which make us human may become the things which tear us into pieces. That is why desires—sexual desires, desires for prosperity, desires for success, desires for good living—all these come like little gods, fighting for the throne; and each one demands to be the king. Intellectual ability may be demanding it should take the throne. Then my affections come rushing in. They want to be the god of my life.

When you become self-centered, you cease to be the man or the woman God meant you to be, and you become a battlefield. That is what our psychologists are telling us these days: split personalities. What splits them? What is it that splits us into pieces? These evil things which defile man do not come out of physical discomforts. Jesus said they come out of the heart. The heart of a man whose self has become its own center becomes a battlefield. He becomes a victimized human being, and sin has a feast when self is the center.

BATTLEFIELD

Of course, I cannot manage myself. I was not created for that purpose. God knew better. He created us in His image, which means He was the Reality inside the image. As soon as He is not in the center of the image, what remains is a battlefield. This is the terrible sin from which all other sins have come. The arena is confused.

There is a toy which children call the spinning top. It is a thing with a big head and a very thin bottom, and because the head is big and the bottom thin, it cannot stand. To make it stay up, you spin it at a terrific speed. You know, there are spinners all over the world, and they can spin round from one thing to another. Our young people these days, and old people too, spin from business after business, success after success. Even study can become spinning.

I have also met Christians who are spinning round chasing butterflies. They cannot settle down. No sooner are they there than they want to be somewhere else. They never settle down. And of course the Holy Spirit has a rough time getting them settled. You cannot catch them. It takes mighty grace to bring them together.

This was the miserable existence Paul knew. Paul was a Jew, a trained Pharisee, a religious man of Israel, who took his religion seriously. He was trained to think. He had sat at the feet of Gamaliel, and he knew the teaching of the rabbis. He understood that when life becomes its own center, it runs in those meaningless circles, because a spinning top never gets anywhere. It goes round and round itself.

Life is no life until it has direction, until it finds its base. Paul says, "We cannot escape from the love of Christ." When the love of Christ comes, it is God intervening in this miserable humdrum of dry repetition, in this dry experience of religion. And then God comes in. Talk about morality, talk about standards, talk about anything we like; as long as I am the center, that life of mine will never know what it means to live. It will simply exist in those meaningless circles all the time, until Jesus comes.

But Christ the Liberator comes to give a humanity which has lost its center a new meaningful center. Life remains meaningless until it finds a center other than itself. Oh, the misery of being a slave of yourself! For when you are a slave of yourself, you are blind. Everyone else is wrong except you. There is no good teaching except what teases your fancy. There is no right church except the one of your choosing. Nothing is good in the world unless it pleases you. What a miserable life!

The whole world is full of men and women who are slaves of themselves. We need the Liberator to liberate us from this meaningless circle, this business of making myself the center.

POWERFUL LOVE

Paul says, "You know, we can no longer escape." Have you been trying to run away? The love of Christ is so powerful that it grabbed Paul on the road to Damascus, and instead of sending him in circles of confusion, it so released him that for the rest of his life he was a man with one direction: "For to me to live is Christ, and to die is gain." At the cross, death lost its vitality; its threat was no longer there. The gates of splendor opened wide. The Son of God took the place of the miserable sinners and introduced a completely liberating center.

How did He do it? In a very costly way. It cost Him blood and sweat, nakedness and shame. And He did it beautifully. It had never happened before; and since it happened, believe me, the world has never been the same. Our world has experienced the greatest epoch in the history of the human race, for God has gained the center. What was His purpose? That men may no longer live for themselves, but for Him. There is new direction, a liberated humanity, and anyone who has found Christ, finds Him an exciting person to live for. I want to tell you, every time I touch on that I am at a loss for words—that humanity should discover the new direction; and the direction came in that practical love, which loved and loved and loved until it died, and in dying it changed the course of history, bringing slaves into liberty.

There is no greater power than the love of God experienced in a believer. You come to that cross, and sin becomes a hundred times more sinful. In the exposure of Christ's redeeming love, a flood of light sheds its rays into the dark heart, and the heart sings: "at the cross, a trembling soul, love and mercy found me." Of course there was the trembling experience. Of course I was afraid. Of course I was a victim of myself. But, you know, those arms embraced me, and then the rays were shed round me at the cross, for love and mercy had found me there.

The purpose is that men should no longer be living to themselves; for if you live to yourself or for yourself, you simply empty yourself. This is why people are running round burning buildings and turning over cars. What are they seeking? In France, there were riots among young people: "We want to live. We want to live"—burn the cars. "We want to live"—smash the buildings. "We want to live"—where can we live? They want to live, but they have not discovered that when you live for yourself you become empty. You hate life. Talk about the sexual immorality which has invaded succeeding generations! What is its purpose? It is living on desire, and therefore emptying desire, so that in the end what remains is an empty shell. Money can create an empty shell, too.

BRINGS LIFE

Jesus came that men and women may now begin to live—and live to Him and for Him who died and rose again for them. The resurrection was a seal that He had accomplished a mighty work for you and me. Our liberation was sealed with His own blood. It was witnessed when He rose from the dead, and it was made actual when the Holy Spirit came down on the day of Pentecost. Glorious! What did the Spirit come to give? Some people think He came to give certain spiritual gifts. Those are too small. They are part of the blessing, but they are too small to meet the whole crying need in life. He came to bring the risen Lord, the One who died, and to enthrone Him in the heart of the believer, so that the heart which was in darkness is flooded with light, and flooded with liberty, because the Liberator is inside.

We find we no longer have the same values. As soon as you stand in the presence of that Liberator, your values and your goals change. Before the experience, you looked at men as Africans, Chinese, Indians, poor, rich, and so on. When you come to the cross, they are all changed. You see in the face of every man written clearly, "For this one Christ died." You can no longer treat them as foreigners or cases.

SOUTH AFRICA

What is the real problem in South Africa? It is not that that whites in South Africa hate the blacks. It is that the minority is scared of the majority. They see threatening shadows peeping into their material gains, and are scared, and so fences of security go up! The masses of the "have-nots" are curious to find what lies inside the fences. If the crowds were allowed to come in, it would not be long before they discovered that there was not much there, anyway! But, of course, we are so scared. We are all the time protecting ourselves. But Paul says the cross changes our values. We see men in a completely new light, and they have a new preciousness.

When God acted in Christ on the cross, He stretched out His arms to embrace an unembraceable world, a world of haters. He speaks to every sinner that has ever lived: "You, too, I love."

When you come into His presence, the cross sets you free. The cross gives you a new direction, and the Liberator says, "You can begin to live for Me and not for yourself; and in living for Me you begin to live for yourself. You are accepted intimately, and you can accept yourself." Then men are brothers. The world is no longer a threat. Experiences are taken and used for the glory of God.

An African Christian stood before soldiers with their guns ready to shoot him for his faith, and he sang a hymn. Heaven opened as the brother was shot, but the testimony is still continuing. He took a miserable and terrible experience and used it to glorify the Lord. This is what the Holy Spirit does.

A mission of reconciliation is also given to us. Imagine it! The world is torn with miserable hatreds and resentments. It is corroded and paralyzed, and God says, "I have acted to bring that man to myself, and I am giving you the responsibility of taking the message to him."

Christians have the key. If only you knew you have the key. I want to tell you humbly, I know, though vaguely, I have the God-given key. It is marked with the blood of His Son. It is love, almighty love, which when it meets a corroded personality recreates it. In times of revival, men and women catch a fresh vision of what happened when Jesus shed His blood. That wonderful, mighty love shed abroad on Calvary's cross in the blood of the Son of God whispers messages of forgiveness. As that comes in, you find you want to embrace all humanity.

BARRIERS BROKEN

I shall never forget my experience when God began to break through those circles and fences and barriers which I had put up. I am black. I did not like the white people. I did not like the British because they were ruling us. Then Christ intervened. He knew I was all tied in knots. You see, when you resent other people, you are no longer the same. You no longer live, until you begin to experience the love of God. He came into the world and set this prisoner free. Then he told me, "You go and see a brother"—and that "brother" was an English missionary.

I shall never forget the experience, because it was the beginning. I have had many more, and I am still to have a lot more. But the words which shook me were, "He is your brother, white and English as he is!" This may not make sense to you, but it really shook me. And He told me why. He said, "I died for him, and I died for you, and when you hated Me, I loved you; and you hated that man, so now you go to him."

I did not have a car, but I cycled fifty miles to go to the missionary on Saturday. What was I going to do? Not to preach. I went to ask for forgiveness, and to rediscover my dear brother, as a liberated person.

I remember coming near his house, and a trembling fear got hold of me, and I began even to hope he was not at home. But when I came in and I saw my brother, there stood before me a man whom Jesus loved, and we really had a wonderful time. I embraced him, showing him what had happened.

We stood there, and I asked him to forgive me. That dear man! He loved me, and we stood there, two of us in the presence of the Liberator, our hearts beating in tune—not an Englishman and an African, but born-again believers, set free by the Son of God. We talked, we prayed, and we sang. It is now thirty-three years, and I love him very much still.

Maybe you need to begin to experience in a deeper way the ministry written in the blood of reconciliation. A wounded world can never be healed except by a wounded hand. When love fears to bleed, it ceases to bless. May this be your time to experience the Liberator. God bless you.

CHAPTER 6

ALL THINGS
ARE YOURS

The Apostle Paul wrote to the Corinthian Christians and told them, "All things are yours" (I Corinthians 3:21).

Does that sound rather too big? "All things belong to you." What does he mean? We feel like asking, "Paul, can't you be a little more specific? Wouldn't you like to tell me exactly what those things are?"

You know the Holy Spirit is very gracious. The Holy Spirit tells us exactly what these things are. He gives you a blank check, "All things are yours." Now there is no limit. Heaven is the limit.

When you come to Jesus, there is no limit—you can possess everything He has. The only limit is your unbelief.

Other than your unbelief, there is no limit to His grace for you. You can possess and possess more and more.

But how?

Some of you say, "I am not fit."

It is not a question of being fit. No one has ever been fit. It is a completely different question. It is whether you have been brought into the wonderful new relationship with God by grace. If you have, all things are yours. What is the criterion? Where do we base our possessing? On the fact of belonging to Christ. You can never have anything to do with those blessings until you belong to Christ. Then you are re-possessed by Christ; therefore, you possess.

POSSESSED BY CHRIST

If you are not possessed by Christ, you may as well forget it. Nothing will ever belong to you. You do not even belong to yourself until you belong to Christ. That is why you keep falling apart and keep asking, "Why? Why can't I control myself?" Because you do not belong to yourself until you belong to Christ. You do not have the capacity to possess yourself until you are possessed by the Spirit of God. It is when Christ takes a life into His wonderful hands that He gives that life the ability to possess itself, to guide and control its lusts and desires and temper. Many of us wonder, "How on earth can I put my pieces together?" Who can? As you did not create yourself, you cannot re-create yourself either. But, by belonging to Christ, you belong to yourself.

Being possessed by Christ, you possess life.

Paul says, "All things belong to you." What things? All your teachers. All the teachers in America belong to you. Let me explain. Many Christians think, "I was taught by so-and-so, so I belong to him." You've made a mistake. All teachers belong to you—Apollos, Paul, Peter. Also, your possessions belong to you. There are many people who think they possess what they have—their wealth. But often it is they who belong to their possessions! It is not until Christ possesses you that you begin to possess the world. Then you begin to possess your possessions, your home, your car, your business, your married life.

Young people, do you know you can't possess your life until Christ possesses you? Then He gives you ability to possess your life as a young person. Those who are older and have responsibility, do you realize you will never possess your homes until you are given the ability by the Spirit of God to possess the kind of life you have? This is what the Spirit does for Christians. He doesn't take them out of the world and put them in the clouds. He enables them to live—where they are. And they can live anywhere. By "living" I don't mean mere "existing," these are two different things. But you are given the ability to cope—and the world belongs to you.

Life belongs to you, or does it? How many of you can say, "Yes, life belongs to me"?

Which means, "I can cope with life!" Do you really possess life? Or are you possessed by circumstances? Do you know why we are continually breaking up in life? Because we don't have the ability to possess anything. How many people are breaking under the load of life! Life has become so heavy.

But Paul says, "The world belongs to you if you belong to Christ." Life belongs to you. You possess life. You can cope with it. You can live! And not only that, death belongs to you. How many people possess death? Now this may sound a bit too high. It isn't! If you are a Christian, you can look death in the eyes and wave to it!

NOT AFRAID TO DIE

I have seen Africans who know they are going to die in a few hours. The doctor has said they have only a few hours. They are going to die, and they know it. You can look into their eyes, and there is no sign of death whatsoever. I have seen a friend waving before he died. Waving as if he were going on a journey!—going Home!

The future is ours. How many of us are scared of the future because it spells out weakness, loss of a job, and retirement. Many of us think too much about security. It's good to think about security, but are you secure in your security? Or do you become possessed by your security so that in the end security becomes a prison in which you live? But the present and the future belong to you, because you belong to Christ, and Christ belongs to God, and therefore you are in command.

Possess! Possess! Be free to live.

Recently, we have been having some confusion in a certain country called

Burundi. You may have read about it in your newspapers, how people, precious people, men and women and boys and girls, have died in their thousands, slaughtered by their own people because of political confusion and fighting between one particular class and another. We have lost many, many people. In my church we have lost 18 pastors, not because they had anything to do with that government, but they were caught in the confusion. Christians live in the world, and you can be caught in a confusion to which you have made no contribution.

Let me ask you, what do you do when you are caught in such circumstances? Succumb? Sit down and mourn about it? Lose your testimony? Lose your joy? Let me tell you what some of these Africans have done, when caught in this shock.

SHOCK ABSORBERS

They were living with the Lord Jesus Christ, and therefore when shocks came, they had shock absorbers! There are many people who, when a shock comes, they hit bottom like an old car. They can't take those bumps and humps. But when Christians are in the Spirit, they are given that ability to take the bumps of life without breaking.

One of these men in the midst of this terrible, bloody massacre was a young school teacher. He was called out of his school and told by a firing squad of soldiers, "We are going to shoot you because you are dangerous to our regime."

He looked at them. This was a man in his thirties with a wife and children, and he was going to be shot.

They said, "Have you a word to say before we shoot you?"

He said, "Yes, I have."

"What is it?"

"I LOVE YOU."

Now, this may sound very easy when you are sitting comfortably in your room, but can you imagine yourself saying that with five men in front of you with guns about to shoot you? And you look into their faces and say, "I—love—you."

Can they forget that word? Are you surprised? Is it sentimentality when a gun is pointed at you? It is a tough experience. But this young man is the master of his situation. These men are going to shoot, but he can look in their faces and say, "I love you!" They are dumbfounded. They don't know what to say because he is in command. All things are yours.

Then he said, "May I sing a song to you before you shoot me?" And he started to sing: "Out of my bondage, sorrow and night, Jesus, I come! Jesus, I come!"

He sang all four verses in his mother tongue, finishing with that refrain, "Jesus, I come! Jesus, I come!"

His eyes were absolutely full of glory, and his heart was overflowing with the grace of Jesus. And the soldiers noticed it. They saw it clearly. All things are yours—even death, and the world, and even confusion. All things are yours.

When he was through singing, the soldiers, I am told (and they told me the story), for a short time did not know what to do. They had their fingers on the triggers of their guns, but they couldn't move. How do you shoot a man who is singing, beaming with joy, and going Home anyway? Your shooting is absolutely meaningless. If the prisoner were angry, you could say, "I've done a good job," but here he is—he is almost saying to you, "Send me Home quickly!"

So in the end they did their miserable duty; they shot the man. And he died. But really, did he die? Can they ever forget the joy? Can they ever forget those words, "Jesus, I come!" Can they say it was phony—just Christians in a church? It was outside in the open, somewhere in a lonely spot, before a gun. This is true Christianity. This is the meaning of: "All things are yours." If that young African could master his situation, let me ask you, are you in command in your situation?

IN COMMAND

What situation is tearing you apart? You feel so weak, you don't know what to do. And here is another Christian brother of yours. He is about to be shot, which is a harder experience than yours, and he is leaving a wife and children behind. He is being shot unjustly, and yet he is in command. Are you in command?

If you are not in command, I will tell you why. You are not in focus with Jesus Christ. You are in focus perhaps, with your own self. You are focused upon your desires and circumstances. You look at your psychological and mental capacities and problems. This is not where you get the help. If you are going to be in command in your life in the present and future, life, death, teachers, and problems, then you have to ask the Spirit of God to refocus your attention upon what Jesus is and what He did.

You come into focus—into direct attention—when by the Spirit of God you are taken to the cross where a helpless person who was hanging alone on a piece of wood became the Redeemer of the entire world. Since He died on that cross and rose again, the world has never been the same. I don't mean that the world has accepted Him. If it did, it would be a completely different world—there would never be these miserable confusions of racial, tribal, and national massacres and wars. You know every day in your newspapers there is a war—there is the report that somebody has killed somebody—that's war.

Why is it happening? Because Jesus said, "Out of the hearts of men and women," not out of Burundi but out of the hearts of people—"come murders, jealousies, hatreds, lusts, wrong desires, and greed." They all come out of the heart. Wherever you have the hearts of people, that's what comes out until Jesus Christ comes in. And He comes in by way of the cross. At the cross, we meet

the wonderful God in human body, suffering in pain, and at the same time in command. Suffering with nails in His hands—
He can't move—He's in pain, He's treated
unjustly, but He's in command. When a
Christian comes by way of the cross, he is
given ability by the Holy Spirit to cope with
all the nasty experiences of life.

May God bless you as you receive this
tremendous ability to cope with circumstances. All things are yours. Can you take
those circumstances in which you are and
say, "Even my situation belongs to me"?
Yes, even yours.

A few years ago, I had flown from Brit-
ain and had stopped at the international
airport in my country and was going to
be joined by other brethren going to a convention across Lake Victoria. I waited for
these dear men to come and join me, so

that we could go, but they were not to be seen anywhere. I tried to telephone, but could not get through. In the end, I got in the plane alone, and went, not knowing what had happened.

Two days later, when I was in Tanzania, I got a letter from my daughter, and this is what she said: "On the eve of the 24th, our brethren were at the bus terminal with their baggage ready to go to the convention 700 miles away. Others were seeing them off. Somehow a group of soldiers came and arrested them, rounding them up quickly, men and women, and threw them into a military jail. While you were waiting at the airport, the ones you waited for were in jail."

Two days later, they were released because there had been a confusion, but let me tell you this. They had been heading for a Christian gathering to have a wonderful time to sing together, pray together, praise God, and lead others to Christ. Instead, they found themselves in a jail. That's not what they had planned. What do you do then? Sit there? Become critical and bitter? Become hard?

These Christians, as soon as they were thrown into jail, began with great peace to take over the whole place, soldiers and all. They started witnessing immediately. They took out their Bibles and were not stopped from reading them. Soldiers became interested. They sang and praised. I believe the jail was like a church, except a little warmer than ordinary churches.

For two days, those soldiers were exposed to the most wonderful atmosphere. Men and women praising, singing, reading, praying, loving them, shaking their hands. When the President said, "All right, let them out, it was not their fault," and they were freed, I am told every officer in that jail, and their wives, came and lined up to shake the hands of these Christian men and women and wave as they left. When I heard the story, I was very jealous that I wasn't with them! They got out, but, in danger and uncertainty, all things were theirs. They took over. It was confusion, it was painful, it was unjust, but those soldiers will never forget them—never forget the love and the freedom, the joy, and liberty which they saw.

It's an exciting thing to preach the Gospel under such circumstances because you don't know what to expect. All you know is that Jesus is there, and He has given you something precious to share and you are sharing it.

So I want to finish by asking you, are you in command of whatever situation you are in at present? Remember, "All things are yours."

ABOUT THE AUTHOR

Festo Kivengere (ki-VEN-jə-rā) was the Anglican Bishop of the diocese of Kigezi in Uganda. He was the founder and leader of African Enterprise's East Africa teams in Kenya, Tanzania, and Uganda.

Forced to flee for his life from Uganda in 1977 at the height of Idi Amin's eight-year reign of terror, Festo and his wife, Mera, remained abroad until the liberation of his country in 1979. He then immediately returned home to bring the message of God's reconciling love in Jesus Christ to his shattered homeland. Through African Enterprise, he helped organize emergency relief for those who were suffering and long-term help for the reconstruction of Uganda.

Deeply influenced by the East African Revival—one of the great movements of the Spirit in the last century—Festo Kivengere's ministry of reconciliation crosses boundaries of race, culture and denomination. Many regarded him as the outstanding black evangelist of Africa in his day, and the impact of his ministry is felt around the world.

For his courageous stand on freedom and human rights in Africa, Festo received the International Freedom Prize in October 1977 in Oslo, Norway. And for his significant ministry to the Christian community worldwide, he was awarded in 1981 the St. Augustine Cross by the Archbishop of Canterbury.

Festo Kivengere is the author of *Revolutionary Love* (also published by CCM Books), *Love Unlimited*, *When God Moves*, *I Love Idi Amin*, and *Hope for Uganda*. Festo died of leukemia May 18, 1988 in Nairobi, Kenya.